life and that _____
(though I can _____
a degree). However, I know
He holds your tears and
blends them with His own
tears shed for you and He
will comfort you and He
is there with you. So I
pray that these things
will begin to seep in through
the dark hours you endure
and immerse you in
more and more of His
love and light.
        Bless you, Kris!
            I love you dearly.
        Love,
            Cheryl

To:

Kris

THE LORD YOUR GOD IS
WITH YOU ... HE WILL QUIET
YOU WITH HIS LOVE.
ZEPHANIAH 3:17

From:

Cheryl November 17, 05

🌿

Compiler: Londa P. Alderink
Associate Editor: Molly Detweiler
Design Manager: Amy E. Langeler
Designer: Amy Peterman

All artwork is copyrighted by Joni Eareckson Tada.

Printed in China
02 03 04/HK/ 5 4 3 2 1

God's Tender Care

JONI
EARECKSON TADA

inspirio™

The gift group of Zondervan

IF YOU'RE MEETING JONI FOR THE FIRST TIME...

Joni Eareckson Tada, as the result of a diving accident, has lived in a wheelchair, paralyzed from the shoulders down, for over thirty years. "So many actions, sensations, thoughts, and feelings were crowded into that fragment of time," Joni recalls about the accident. She continues, "I recall so clearly the details of those few dozen seconds—seconds destined to change my life forever. And there was no warning or premonition.

"What happened on July 30, 1967, was the beginning of an incredible adventure which I feel compelled to share because of what I have learned." And in a quest to better understand the goodness of God in the midst of suffering, she has invested most of the past thirty plus years in a probing and personal study of God's Word.

The following pages are testimonies of only a fraction of what she has come to learn, believe, and know about the grace God extends to those who trust in Him in the middle of trying circumstances. As Joni has said before, "I have found that God knows my needs infinitely better than I know them. And He is utterly dependable, no matter which direction our circumstances take us."

Joni's prayer is that you will experience God's tender care and grace during your time of struggle, not as she has, but in a way that is unique to your own situation.

May God be with you on the journey ahead.

STRENGTH ...
WHILE YOU WAIT

Those who hope in the LORD
will renew their strength.
They will soar on wings like eagles;
they will run and not grow weary,
they will walk and not be faint.

ISAIAH 40:31

Years ago my family and I took a camping trip up into the wilderness reserve of Jasper Provincial Park in Alberta, Canada. I remember boarding a chairlift that cabled us to the top of a huge, glacier-scared mountain overlooking a broad expanse of pine forest below. There I marveled at the sight of a soaring eagle moving far across the wooded valley—just a tiny speck against the distant mountain range. I watched as the eagle circled and dove, admiring his grace and ease.

Eagles seem to go with big things—mountains, canyons, great depths, immense heights. It's always at the most stupendous and alluring spectacles of nature that we find them.

God talks about eagles. In one of the best-loved passages of the Old Testament, Isaiah 40:30-31, He uses their flight to describe the adventure that will unfold to the suffering Christian who waits for Him.

Most of us think of "waiting" as passive, something we have to do before the "real action" begins, a wearisome means to a better end. We wait in line at the grocery checkout counter, watch the clock on the wall at the dentist's office, glance at our watch while in a bank teller's line.

But waiting on God is far different. It's not passive, it's active. And it's not as though we *first* wait and *then* finally get the chance to mount up with wings, run without tiring, and walk without weariness. No, those good things actually happen while we are *waiting*! Waiting on God is an active, confident trusting ... an instant obedience.

Isaiah promises a new and exciting perspective when we wait on the Lord. Waiting on God gives us the kind of perspective that an eagle must have. Our surroundings come into focus. Our horizons are broadened. We see our place in the scheme of things.

Waiting on God means confidently trusting that God knows how much I need and can take. It means looking expectantly toward the time when He will free me from my burdens. God's promise is clear. Those who wait for Him in their distress will receive strength and endurance which others know nothing about.

My body is now held by the limits of this wheelchair. But the waiting hope I have in God's future for me gives me the freedom to soar to heights of joy and explore the canyon depths of God's tender mercies.

All in all, it's worth the wait.

RESTING
IN HIS ARMS

*A*h, a child's life, wrapped in a warm blanket, sleeping peacefully in his mother's arms, with hardly a care in the world. Worries aren't his responsibility. A baby seems to know that mother will always be close by tending to every need. No wonder a baby sleeps soundly.

Do you ever wish that your life were like that? Flip through the pictures of baby Jesus on your Christmas cards, sleeping peacefully, and you might think, "If only my life were that simple."

God has a reminder for you. As a mother comforts her child, so will I comfort you. (Isaiah 66:13)

That's an odd description for our heavenly Father, but God paints this tender picture in order to make an important point. He wants to remind you that His breast is a place of comfort. In Him, you can be satisfied. You, too, can rest peacefully knowing that Someone will always be close to you, tending to every need. The Lord is your father, friend, husband, and brother. And according to Isaiah 66, He is also your mother. He is everything to you, just as a parent is to a child.

So when everything seems a little out of control, a little crazy, if you are feeling the heavy burdens of being an adult, take a moment to talk to the Lord as would a child. He longs to pick you up and wrap you tenderly in His care. And in His arms, you can daily find rest.

Hear, O LORD, and answer me,
  for I am poor and needy.
Guard my life, for I am devoted to you.
  you are my God; save your servant who trusts in you.
Have mercy on me, O LORD,
  for I call to you all day long.
Bring joy to your servant,
  for to you, O LORD,
  I lift up my soul.

PSALM 86:1-4

Cast all your anxiety on God because he cares
  for you.

I PETER 5:7

*J*esus said, "I will do whatever you ask in my name, so that the Son may bring glory to the Father. You may ask me for anything in my name, and I will do it.

I tell you the truth, if anyone says to this mountain, 'Go, throw yourself into the sea,' and does not doubt in his heart but believes that what he says will happen, it will be done for him. Therefore I tell you, whatever you ask in prayer, believe that you will receive it, and it will be yours."

JOHN 14:13-14; MARK 11:23-24

CLAY AND WAX

O LORD, you are our Father.
We are the clay, you are the potter;
we are all the work of your hand.

ISAIAH 64:8

I recall visiting a sculptor's studio. She was working on several designs, large lumps of clay, covered with damp cheesecloth. The clay could readily harden if the humidity or temperature in her studio changed even slightly.

But not so with the wax my sculptor friend used in designing pieces for reproduction. It remained soft and pliable, easy to work with. Whenever she wanted to create a work of art, she would warm the wax with a hair dryer and it was immediately ready.

Hardened clay is brittle. If dropped, it can fracture into a thousand pieces. Dropped wax, however, only bends from the pressure of the fall and can be quickly remolded.

People are like that too. Those who bend to the will of God find perfect expression in however God molds them.

I thought of these things some time back when I was in bed, depressed, as a result of a pressure sore. For three months I struggled to remain pliable and open to God's will. In one of those mad, midnight moments during my long convalescence, teetering between a hardened clay and a melted wax response, I came up with a song...

I have a piece of china, a pretty porcelain vase.

  It holds such lovely flowers, captures everyone's gaze

  But fragile things do slip and fall as everybody knows

  And when my days came crashing down, my tears began to flow.

  But don't we all cry when pretty things get broken,

    Don't we all cry at such an awful loss?

    But Jesus will dry your tears as He has spoken

    'Cause He was the one broken on the cross.

My life was just like china, a lovely thing to me,

Full of porcelain promises of all that I might be.

But fragile things do slip and fall, as everybody knows,

And when my vase came crashing down, my tears began to flow.

But Jesus is no porcelain prince, His promises won't break.

His holy work holds fast and sure, His love no one can shake.

So if your life is shattered by sorrow, pain, or sin,

His healing love will reach right down and make you whole again.

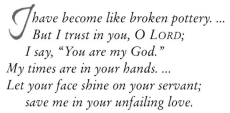

I *have become like broken pottery. ...*
*But I trust in you, O L*ORD*;*
I say, "You are my God."
My times are in your hands. ...
Let your face shine on your servant;
save me in your unfailing love.

PSALM 31:12, 14-16

*B*e still, and know that I am God.

PSALM 46:10

*L*et us approach the throne of grace with confidence, so that we may receive and find grace to help us in our time of need.

HEBREWS 4:16

*J*esus said, "My grace is sufficient for you, for my power is made perfect in weakness."

2 CORINTHIANS 12:9

HAND-TAILORED
HARDSHIPS

*H*ave you ever looked at someone going through a tough time and thought, *Boy, I'm glad that's not me. I could never handle that situation.* Sure you have. I have, too. And I'll tell you someone else who thinks that: my friend Charlene. She was recently in the hospital, having temporarily lost control of her muscles. She had to be fed and had to wear an indwelling catheter. That meant no trips to the bathroom (she carried her bathroom with her) and lots of discomfort.

Charlene later told me, "Joni, I don't know how you do it. I'm glad you're the quadriplegic rather than me. I love my independence."

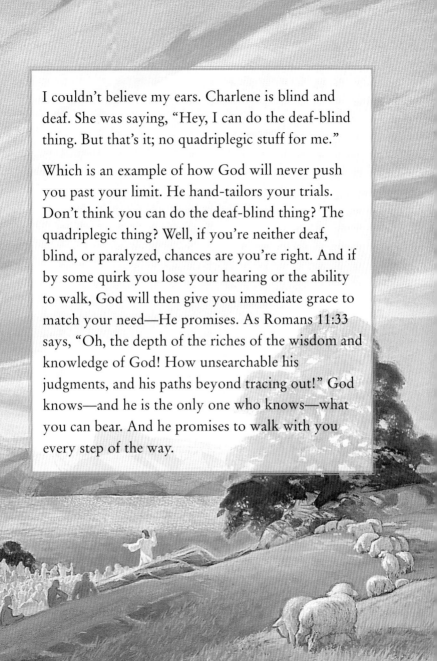

I couldn't believe my ears. Charlene is blind and deaf. She was saying, "Hey, I can do the deaf-blind thing. But that's it; no quadriplegic stuff for me."

Which is an example of how God will never push you past your limit. He hand-tailors your trials. Don't think you can do the deaf-blind thing? The quadriplegic thing? Well, if you're neither deaf, blind, or paralyzed, chances are you're right. And if by some quirk you lose your hearing or the ability to walk, God will then give you immediate grace to match your need—He promises. As Romans 11:33 says, "Oh, the depth of the riches of the wisdom and knowledge of God! How unsearchable his judgments, and his paths beyond tracing out!" God knows—and he is the only one who knows—what you can bear. And he promises to walk with you every step of the way.

JESUS THE
PROMISE KEEPER

*You know with all your heart and soul that
not one of all the good promises the LORD
your God gave you has failed. Every promise
has been fulfilled; not one has failed.*

JOSHUA 23:14

*H*e stood out in a crowd—a tall, handsome,
black man from Jamaica with a big smile.
I saw him shaking people's hands and heard each
person tell him how encouraging his testimony was.
As the crowd thinned, I wheeled up to him, leaned
forward, and lifted my arm, a hint to let him know I
wanted to shake hands. He smiled and leaned
forward to extend his hand. Then a surprising thing
happened: I realized he had no hands. This joyful
Christian wore black fiberglass hands. We
commented that even though we couldn't feel it,
our "handshake" sure looked good!

He smiled broadly and said, "Sister, aren't you glad
we have Jesus? We have his promises!" Jesus and his
promises. They are virtually one and the same.

This disabled man from a poor country has staked his life on God's promises. His promise to lead. To sustain. To protect and provide. To meet every need. And he does so because he loves Jesus. As 2 Corinthians 1:20 says, "no matter how many promises God has made, they are 'Yes" in Christ." To believe in Christ is to believe in God's promises.

Father, help me to sink my anchor deep in your promises. As life's waves broadside my boat, enable me to remember that every promise has its beginning and ending in Jesus.

The LORD is good,
*   a refuge in times of trouble.*
He cares for those who trust in him.

NAHUM 1:7

God is able to make all grace abound to you, so that in
*   all things at all times, having all that you need, you*
will abound in every good work.

2 CORINTHIANS 9:8

The LORD *longs to be gracious to you;*
he rises to show you compassion.
For the LORD *is a God of justice.*
Blessed are all who wait for him.

ISAIAH 30:18

The LORD *will fulfill his purpose for me;*
your love, O LORD, *endures forever.*

PSALM 138:8

GRACE: FRESH DAILY

Not long ago I was looking through a *National Geographic* magazine and came across an article on the Sinai wilderness. Page after page showed photos of a dry wasteland. Vegetation amounted to a few scrub bushes here and there and an occasional lonely palm.

It prompted me to think about the forty years the nation Israel wandered in the wilderness after the exodus from Egypt. The Bible tells us that the main staple of their diet during that time was a flaky foodstuff called "manna."

They ate that stuff for forty years. Can you imagine? They must have outdone Julia Child in thinking of 101 ways to make manna taste different. Yet it was food. It was life. And it was necessary for them to gather it fresh every morning before it could melt away in the heat of the noonday sun.

There were times during a twelve-week stay in bed that I wondered how I would continue. I'd get depressed just thinking about the remaining weeks I needed to stay out of my wheelchair.

It's been said that grace is the desire and the power to do God's will. Well, I lacked both. It was clear that this grace, this gift, was going to have to come from God. And as a gift, it's something for which I had to ask.

James tells us the asking must be done in humility. "God opposes the proud, " he writes, "but gives grace to the humble" (James 4:6). At that point I wasn't having trouble with pride. I had come to a place where I was broken, humbled, even humiliated by my lack of ability. Yet my mind was locked up with worry over the future.

Numb with anxiety, I finally came across verses from Lamentations Chapter 3 which unlocked my spirit: "For His compassions never fail. They are new every morning" (vv. 22-23). In other words, the grace God gives you and me today is sufficient *for today only*. Just like the Israelites, I needed to wake up in the morning, go out, and gather a day's supply. It was no good trying to stockpile grace for the long, hungry days ahead.

Grace, like manna, can't be stored. It is "new every morning." And God is the wonderful and willing supplier.

Lord, I am thankful that I am your priority today. I recognize that as you've offered yourself to me, I can find my fill for all my needs. And as I find fullness in You, tomorrow's worries and anxieties have no place to reside within me. Thank you, Lord.

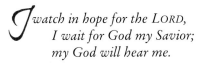

watch in hope for the LORD,
I wait for God my Savior;
my God will hear me.

MICAH 7:7

ou are God my Savior,
and my hope is in you all day long.

PSALM 25:5

SHADOWS

One of my favorite times of the day is late afternoon when shadows steal across our backyard. Ken and I like to pour a cool drink and sit out back, quietly watching the shadows shift and change. We position our chairs in the shade of our neighbor's big pine to escape the heat of the California sun. Trouble is, we have to keep inching our chairs to the left to keep up with that shadow.

Shadows. Always moving, changing with the seasons, shifting with the sun, never constant, never the same. The comfort we seek from them is temporary at best. We find shadows fickle friends.

Ah, but there is Someone who casts an unchanging shadow. James 1:17 tells us that, "Every good and perfect gift is from above, coming down from the Father of the heavenly lights, who does not change like shifting shadows."

Our Father's shadow never shifts because He never changes. He's not evolving, as some theologians would have us believe. He's not transmutable, as other religions profess. No, He is constant and changeless. Always compassionate. Always merciful. Always just. Always holy. Always full of love.

The relief we find in His presence does not change with the passing of the hours, days, or years. The encouragement we find in His promises will not fail us when the heat of adversity bears down upon us. The security we find in His character will never vary though our lives turn upside down and the world changes around us.

How wonderful to have His shadow fall across us. Psalm 91 begins by saying, "He who dwells in the shelter of the Most High will abide in the shadow of the Almighty." The psalmist goes on to detail the many ways God protects His own, making them feel secure. In verses 11-12 we're told, "For he will command his angels concerning you to guard you in all your ways. They will lift you up in their hands so that you will not strike your foot against a stone."

He will never fail you. Place your chair in the shadow of the cross, and you will never have to move it.

Lord, thank you for the perfect and unchanging love and security I can find in you. I know that sometimes I struggle to understand your purpose and plan, but help me to know through it all that you have me, your precious child, in mind and, most importantly, at heart.

The LORD is full of compassion and mercy.

JAMES 5:11

Let us hold unswervingly to the hope we profess, for God who promised is faithful.

HEBREWS 10:23

PRESCRIPTION FOR
WEARINESS

irst Peter 5:7 kept echoing in my mind as I powered my wheelchair through the group of disabled residents in a home for people with cerebral palsy. I clunked wheels with a boy in a bulky, oversized chair while trying to listen to a mentally handicapped girl explain her testimony. Another patient was leaning against the wall, whining to go back to his room.

A nurse wanted me to come and talk to a quadriplegic who was confined to his dormitory. I smiled, nodding at the nurse, and tried to keep my focus on the girl's testimony. It was useless. The nagging whine of the man against the wall shattered what little concentration I had left.

I was far from home and slightly irritated that my sponsors had overloaded my schedule. I had been up all day touring and talking at a rehab center, leading a disability workshop with pastors, and now I was bone-tired. I wanted to scrap the evening, head out the door, and get back to the hotel before they closed the restaurant.

I had to stop. I had to remember that Jesus was with me, moving ahead of my wheelchair, and delighting in the smiles of the faces of each disabled resident. In the midst of the clamor, I discovered His voice, whispering, "Come to me, Joni, you are weary and burdened. Let me give you rest." I paused and prayed silently, asking God to give me His rest. That was all the reminder I needed.

Thank You, Lord, for carrying my cares today!

May our Lord Jesus Christ himself and God our Father, who loved us and by his grace gave us eternal encouragement and good hope, encourage your hearts and strengthen you in every good deed and word.

2 THESSALONIANS 2:16-17

The LORD gives strength to the weary.

ISAIAH 40:29

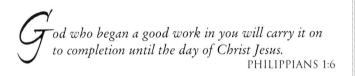

*G*od who began a good work in you will carry it on
  to completion until the day of Christ Jesus.

PHILIPPIANS 1:6

*T*he LORD gives strength to his people;
  the LORD blesses his people with peace.

PSALM 29:11

PRECIOUS JEWELS

They shall be mine, saith the LORD of hosts, in that day when I make up my jewels; and I will spare them, as a man spareth his own son that serveth him.

MALACHI 3:17 KJV

I love for my wedding ring to shine. About once a week I ask my friend who gets me up to use my toothpaste and toothbrush to scrub my ring. Real gold and diamonds can take a good scrubbing; they're not as delicate as we think. And when they're polished, my, they look lovely!

Malachi 3:16-17 talks about how the Lord has a book of remembrance in which the names of all those who meditate on him, who think about his name, are written down. He calls these people his jewels. How do we become jewels that gleam and shine in his sight? He says, "I will refine them like silver and test them like gold. They will call on my name and I will answer them; I will say, 'They are my people,' and they will say, 'The Lord is our God'" (Zechariah 13:9).

Oh, that's what I want to be: a jewel that shines in his sight, a jewel that doesn't mind a good polishing now and then. I'm not as delicate as some people think, especially when God's grace sustains me.

Maybe you feel as if someone has taken a gigantic toothbrush and is scrubbing your soul raw. It hurts. And you wince at the pain, the disappointment. But take heart; there's a purpose. You are someone who is very special to God. You're a diamond, you're silver, and you're gold. He promises that, as his jewel, he's going to shine you up. As silver is refined and as gold is tried, he will polish you bright so everyone will see you're a jewel.

Oh, Lord, the pain is so deep and the hurt I feel cannot be described with words. But I believe that I am special to you and you are going to help me through this so that everyone can see that I am a precious jewel—your precious jewel.

BROKEN CUPS

*But we have this treasure in jars of clay to show that this
all-surpassing power is from God and not from us.*
2 CORINTHIANS 4:7

I was spring-cleaning with a friend the other
day. While reaching into the recesses of the
cupboard, she accidentally dropped a cup. It didn't
shatter, but the fall to the counter was enough to
cause a crack. I wondered whether to save it but in
the end decided to trash.

God, on the other hand, saves broken cups. In fact,
broken vessels are often his most useful tools.
Second Corinthians 4:7 reads like his fix-it manual.
It tells us God pours his treasure into fragile vessels
that are prone to shatter. That way everyone will
know God is doing the living in us.

A broken neck has taught me this. But so has a broken heart. At times, whether in my paralysis pain or emotional pain, I have gone to God, sighing and saying, "I give up. I can't do anything right. I have no idea how to pull myself out of this mess." The world would say, "Yep, you're useless." The Devil would say, "Told you so." But God says, "I've been waiting for you to come to me in your brokenness. Here, let me heal you."

Do not fear, for I am with you;
do not be dismayed, for I am your God.
I will strengthen you and help you;
I will uphold you with my righteous right hand.
ISAIAH 41:10

He will cover you with his feathers,
and under his wings you will find refuge;
his faithfulness will be your shield and rampart.
PSALM 91:4

*T*he LORD *is faithful to all his promises*
and loving toward all he has made.

PSALM 145:13

*M*ay the God of hope fill you with all joy and peace
as you trust in him, so that you may overflow
with hope by the power of the Holy Spirit.

ROMANS 15:13

SHATTERED GLASS

Put your trust in the light while you have it,
so that you may become sons of the light.
JOHN 12:36

My art studio is a mess of half-chewed pastel pencils, old tubes of paint, and piles of illustrations overflowing my file drawers. Recently while cleaning up, I discovered some broken glass on the counter by the window. I also discovered that when sunlight struck the shattered glass, brilliant, colorful rays scattered everywhere.

Shattered glass is full of a thousand different angles, each one picking up a ray of light and shooting it off in a thousand directions. That doesn't happen with plain glass, such as a jar. The glass must be broken into many pieces.

[The angel] carried me away in the Spirit to a mountain great and high, and showed me the Holy City, Jerusalem, coming down out of heaven from God. It shone with the glory of God, and its brilliance was like that of a very precious jewel, like a jasper, clear as crystal.

REVELATION 21:10-11

What's true of shattered glass is true of a broken life. Shattered dreams. A heart full of fissures. Hopes that are splintered. A life in pieces that appears to be ruined. But given time and prayer, such a person's life can shine more brightly than if the brokenness had never happened. When the light of the Lord Jesus falls upon a shattered life, that believer's hopes can be brightened.

It's the nature of things that catch the light: The color and dazzle of light sparkles best through things that are shattered.

hen I am afraid,
*   I will trust in you.*
In God, whose word I praise,
*   in God I trust; I will not be afraid.*

PSALM 56:3-4

Only our great God can reach down into what otherwise would be brokenness and produce something beautiful. With him, nothing is wasted. Every broken dream and heart that hurts can be redeemed by His loving, warm touch. Your life may be shattered by sorrow and pain, but God has in mind a kaleidoscope through which His light can shine more brilliantly.

Light of the world, may You shine today in dark places all over the earth. May broken people, hurt and disappointed, respond to Your loving touch. I present to You the parts of my life that are shattered. Shine, Jesus, shine!

*G*od heals the brokenhearted
and binds up their wounds.

PSALM 147:3

*I*n my anguish I cried to the LORD,
and he answered by setting me free.

PSALM 118:5

You, O Lord, keep my lamp burning;
  My God turns my darkness into light.

PSALM 18:28

I lift up my eyes to the hills—
  where does my help come from?
My help comes from the Lord,
  the Maker of heaven and earth.

PSALM 121:1-2

Let the light of your face shine upon us, O LORD.

PSALM 4:6

The LORD is my rock, my fortress and my deliverer;
my God is my rock, in whom I take refuge.
He is my shield and the horn of my salvation, my
stronghold.
I call to the LORD, who is worthy of praise.

PSALM 18:2-3

SWEET HOUR
OF PRAYER

Sweet hour of prayer, sweet hour of prayer,
That calls me from a world of care,
And bids me at my Father's throne
Make all my wants and wishes known.

God invites us to make all our wants and
wishes known to Him. It's not only a
marvelous invitation, but it's what prayer is
all about. God wants you to tell Him your problems
so that He can comfort you. He wants to hear about
your longings so that He can purify them. Tell Him
about your temptations so that He can help you
conquer them.

Talk to God about everything that's on your heart.
And when you do, remember that prayer is also the
chance to hear the heartbeat of God. He desires to
make known to *you* His wants and wishes.

When you pray this way, you may discover that a
whole hour—an entire hour of sweet communion—
has just flown by. Time races away all too quickly

when you're spending it in intimate conversation
with your dearest friend.

And since He bids me seek His face,
Believe His Word, and trust His grace,
I'll cast on Him my ev'ry care,
And wait for thee, sweet hour of prayer.

Lord, You are my friend and I want to tell You
about my wants and wishes. More so, I want to hear
You share Your heart with me. As I open up Your
Word, speak to me. And as your Spirit opens up my
heart, may my prayer be honest and real.

GOD RUSHES
TO YOUR AID

In my distress I called to the LORD;
I cried to my God for help.
From his temple he heard my voice;
my cry came before him, into his ears.

The earth trembled and quaked,
and the foundations of the mountains shook. ...
He parted the heavens and came down. ...
He mounted the cherubim and flew;
he soared on the wings of the wind.
PSALM 18:6-7, 9-10

When you read this psalm, you are struck by the fact that God moves heaven and earth to come to your aid when you cry to Him for help. At your heartfelt plea, your Lord thunders from heaven and scatters your enemies. Verses 16, 17, and 19 then add, "He reached down from on high and took hold of me; he drew me out of deep

waters. He rescued me from my powerful enemy. ... He brought me out into a spacious place; he rescued me because he delighted in me."

When you pray for God's support, He never is uncaring or unfeeling about your plea. God is not off somewhere on a mountaintop at an arm's length from your cry. When you pray for help, He will not lean over the wall of His ivory tower to tell you to beg louder.

God is attentive to your needs as a caring father is to his dearest son. When you send out a distress call to the Lord, He parts the heavens to come to your rescue.

O Lord, how great is Your compassion
and love toward us!

*C*ast your cares on the LORD
and he will sustain you;
he will never let the righteous fall.

PSALM 55:22

*J*esus said, "Come to me, all you who are weary and
burdened, and I will give you rest."

MATTHEW 11:28

O ne thing God has spoken,
*   two things have I heard:*
that you, O God, are strong,
*   and that you, O Lord, are loving.*

PSALM 62:11-12

T he LORD is near to all who call on him,
*   to all who call on him in truth.*

PSALM 145:18

HIGHS AND
LOWS

*After six days Jesus took Peter, James and
John with him and led them up a high mountain,
where they were all alone. There he was
transfigured before them.*

MARK 9:2

*Then Jesus returned to his disciples and
found them sleeping.*

MARK 14:37

Does it mystify you that one day you can
be on top of the world, in love with the
Lord, soaring in his Spirit, having faith to see far
into eternity, and the next day you go splat? You
find yourself at rock bottom, your faith dried up,
your spirit as dull as dishwater.

It happens to you and it happens to me. And it happened to the Lord's three best friends, Peter, James, and John. In Mark 9 they were on the Mount of Transfiguration. They got an up-close-and-personal, snow-blinded look at the dazzling glory of the Lord as he revealed himself in a way he never had before. They dropped to their knees, jaws agape, dumbstruck with wonder. What ecstasy!

Now, you would think that experience would carry the disciples for years to come. But a short time later in the Garden of Gethsemane, Jesus revealed another

part of himself. He showed them how deeply distressed and troubled he was. You know what happened next: Peter, James, and John yawned, then hit rock bottom. All that spiritual get-up-and-go got up and went.

We often do the same. We rise to some new level of spirituality and commit ourselves to a fresh allegiance to the Savior. Then we are bewildered at the depths to which we fall almost the next day.

Don't set yourself up for defeat—glory in his commitment to you. Ask him moment by moment to keep his arms underneath you as you rise to the mountaintop. He is the only one who preserves you as you descend the other side.

As for me, I will always hope; I will praise you more and more.

PSALM 71:14

Lord Jesus, thank you for the wonderful mountaintop experiences when I can witness your power and strength firsthand. But most of all, thank you for your sustaining power and everlasting arms that I can lean on when I'm struggling with my faith in you. I know you will carry me in those weak moments. Thank you, Jesus, thank you.

Though you have not seen Christ, you love him; and even though you do not see him now, you believe in him and are filled with inexpressible and glorious joy, for you are receiving the goal of your faith, the salvation of your souls.

1 PETER 1:8-9

*L*ord, you have been our dwelling place
throughout all generations.
Before the mountains were born
or you brought forth the earth and the world,
from everlasting to everlasting you are God.

PSALM 90:1-2

*B*e strong and take heart,
all you who hope in the LORD.

PSALM 31:24

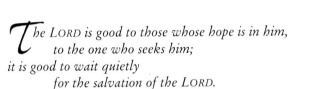

The LORD *is good to those whose hope is in him,*
to the one who seeks him;
it is good to wait quietly
for the salvation of the LORD.

LAMENTATIONS 3:25-26

Be joyful in hope, patient in affliction, faithful in
prayer.

ROMANS 12:12

HEAVEN: WHERE THE
NEGATIVE IS POSITIVE

*D*o you know why a photographer uses a negative to take your photo? He uses it to show us a positive image. It's the same principle when I paint at my easel. Sometimes I choose not to outline a shape, such as a leaf, with a brush, but rather I paint the sky all around the leaf, which then defines its shape. It's called "negative space" painting, and it's a way—some would say a better way—of giving definition to the shapes of leaves against a sky. The artist helps you see by painting what you don't see.

The principle is the same when it comes to heaven: *The negatives are used in order to show us the positive.* On earth, we know all too well what the negatives are: suffering, pain, and death. Show us their opposites, the positive side, and we shall have the best possible idea of the perfect state. For instance, there may be no moon, no marriage, and no need to eat in heaven, as suggested in Revelation 21, but there are also some pretty good *negatives* we can relate to and curiously, they're all listed in Revelation 21 too.

No more sorrow.

No more crying.

No more pain.

No more curse.

And, praise God, no more death.

Selah. Pause. Think of that.

We'd all admit that the sum of human misery on earth vastly outweighs the sum of human happiness. Job said, "Man born of woman is of few days and full of trouble" (14:1). David the psalmist expresses this in Psalm 55:6, 8: "Oh, that I had the wings of a dove! I would fly away and be at rest ... I would hurry to my place of shelter, far from the temptest and storm."

I'm with Job and David: Get me outta here!

Have you ever felt that way? I can't tell you how much sorrow I've held at bay over the years. Tears could come easily if I allowed myself to think of all the pleasures of movement and sensation I've missed. Diving into a pool and feeling my arms and legs slice through the water. Plucking guitar strings with my fingers. Jogging till my muscles burn. To think that one day we shall hear these words uttered that haven't been spoken since Adam was thrust out of Eden: "There shall be no more sorrow."

*Father of heaven and earth, thank you for the
beautiful promises of heaven. Just as you show us
that the negatives of heaven are positives, help me
see the wonderful work you are doing through my
present difficulty. I need you, Lord, I need you.*

*ur light and momentary troubles are achieving for
us an eternal glory that far outweighs them all.
So we fix our eyes not on what is seen, but on what is
unseen. For what is seen is temporary, but what is unseen
is eternal.*

2 CORINTHIANS 4:17-18

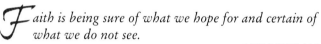

*F**aith is being sure of what we hope for and certain of
what we do not see.*

HEBREWS 11:1

*"W**ith everlasting kindness
          I will have compassion on you,"
says the L*ORD *your Redeemer.*

ISAIAH 54:8

*B*lessed is the man who trusts in the LORD,
 whose confidence is in him.
He will be like a tree planted by the water
 that sends out its roots by the stream.
It does not fear when heat comes;
 its leaves are always green.
It has no worries in a year of drought
 and never fails to bear fruit.

JEREMIAH 17:7-8

GOD WITH US

Isaiah said, "The Lord himself will give you a sign: The virgin will be with child and will give birth to a son, and will call him Immanuel."

ISAIAH 7:14

*I*mmanuel means "God with us." What wonderful words these are! They make all the difference.

Remember those tough days at school? What a relief it was when the teacher showed up at just the right moment to make things right. To stop the talking. To halt the fight. The teacher was in the room and all was well. Whew! So, too, God said he would be with us in the person of Jesus Christ. This mighty promise in the book of Isaiah was fulfilled through Jesus' birth (Matthew 1:22-23).

But that's not all. God was not only going to be here, he would be on our side. Just like the teacher who says, "I'm with you, son. The rest of you, run along."

Life doesn't present itself in a pretty package each day. But we can know that God is with us. He's on our side. So how can we fail? He is ours and he is here.

Lord, I know with you on my side that I can work through any heartache I might experience. Thank you for being on my side.

A ROCK IN A
HIGH PLACE

My family spent the summer of 1959 near a little cow town just north of Phoenix, Arizona. We were helping my Uncle Ted separate his herd of cattle. Each day my sisters and I headed out on the best cow ponies to round up the herds before morning melted into the desert afternoon.

Uncle Ted had told us to head for "the big red boulder up on that yonder ridge" if we ever got lost. One sizzling day I did. I kicked my pony in the boulder's direction and found shelter in the boulder's shadow. It was, for me, a place of refuge.

Within an hour I heard galloping hooves coming up the ridge. I knew I would be found. I knew the high rock had been my certain and only hope.

The same is true for you. No matter how lost you feel, God is with you. If you are resting in him, you are exactly where you're supposed to be. You'll be found. You are safe. Sanctuary in him is only a prayer away.

*Lord, thank you for listening to my prayer.
You are my rock, my strong tower, and I long to
take refuge in the shelter of your wings.*

*I will sing of your strength,
in the morning I will sing of your love;
for you are my fortress,
my refuge in times of trouble.
O my Strength, I sing praise to you;
you, O God, are my fortress, my loving God*

PSALM 59:16-17

*H*ear my cry, O God;
   listen to my prayer.

*From the ends of the earth I call to you,
      I call as my heart grows faint;
      lead me to the rock that is higher than I.
For you have been my refuge,
      a strong tower against the foe.*

*I long to dwell in your tent forever
      and take refuge in the shelter of your wings.*
                                              PSALM 61:1-4

*T*hose who trust in the LORD are like Mount Zion,
  which cannot be shaken but endures forever.

PSALM 125:1

*W*e give thanks to you, LORD God Almighty, the
  One who is and who was, because you have taken
your great power and have begun to reign.

REVELATION 11:17

GOD'S ANGELS

*T*he more heavenly minded I become, the more convinced I am of the presence of angels in my life, whether it's acknowledging their whereabouts in a sports arena or calling them forth to surround the bedside of someone who is sick. Their job description has included bringing messages, aiding in answering prayer and they really shine when it comes to protecting or delivering us. God gets all the credit and glory, but angels mysteriously assist in the process.

Suffice it to say, they're busy.

I'm aware of this every time I drive my handicap-equipped van. Its steering and braking controls are sensitively torqued to accommodate my weak muscles in my shoulders (it doesn't have a steering wheel, but that's another story). When I cruise the Ventura freeway at fifty-five miles per hour, I am keenly conscious of a host of angels surrounding my

van, sitting on the bumper, and holding onto the radio antenna. Maybe God has dispatched an extra few because I'm disabled, and He knows I need extra protection. How many accidents have I avoided because of those angels? When I get to heaven, I'll find out; and I'll thank them for all the times they "lost a few feathers" in near-misses on my behalf.

Lord, especially during these trying times, I thank you for the angels you have watching over me. Praise God that you love me so much.

GOD IS THERE

*G*od, like a good father, doesn't just give
answers. He gives himself. He becomes the
husband to the grieving (Isaiah 54:5). He becomes
the comforter to the barren woman (Isaiah 54:1). He
becomes the father to the orphaned (Psalm 10:14).
He becomes the bridegroom to the single person
(Isaiah 62:5). He is the healer to the sick (Exodus
15:26). He is the Wonderful Counselor to the
confused and depressed (Isaiah 9:6).

This is what you do when someone you love is in anguish: You respond to the plea of their heart by giving them your heart. If you are the One at the center of the universe, holding it together—if everything lives, moves and has its being in you—you can do no more than give yourself (Acts 17:28).

Father, thank you for your presence in my life, especially now. You are my strength.

*B*ecause of his great love for us, God, who is rich in
mercy, made us alive with Christ.

EPHESIANS 2:4-5

*Y*our love, O L*ORD*, reaches to the heavens,
    your faithfulness to the skies.

PSALM 36:5

Praise be to the God and Father of our Lord Jesus Christ, the Father of compassion and the God of all comfort, who comforts us in all our troubles, so that we can comfort those in any trouble with the comfort we ourselves have received from God.

2 CORINTHIANS 1:3-4

A SPARROW MAKES
THE POINT

*So don't be afraid; you are worth more
than many sparrows.*
MATTHEW 10:31

I was just a little girl when my mom and dad
took me to the Baltimore Zoo. But there is
one part of that visit I will never forget.

For some reason, the aviary seized my attention
more than the elephants, monkeys, and giraffes put
together. A large bird exhibition, it was aflutter with
fascinating feathered creatures ... brightly colored
parrots, funny-looking toucans, huge, stern eagles,
and know-it-all owls. But flittering around the
outside of all the cages were common sparrows,
making their homes in the rafters of the aviary.

They weren't important enough to put in a cage for everyone to admire and ogle. They didn't rate an explanatory plaque. Their pictures didn't appear in the zoo guidebook. Mostly, they weren't even noticed.

Yet of all the birds He created, God chose the sparrow to make a crucial point on the subject of fear. Jesus knows how vulnerable we feel at times. How weak mentally, how frail emotionally. A surprising number of us let our apprehensions press us to the edge of our mental limits every once in a while.

Just recently I was there. That's when I came across our Lord's little lecture on sparrows. Jesus was speaking to His men about future events. When He read the fear rising in their hearts, He paused to reassure them. "Are not two sparrows sold for a penny? Yet not one of them will fall to the ground apart from the will of your Father. And even the very hairs of your head are all numbered. So don't be afraid; you are worth more than many sparrows" (Matthew 10:29-31).

How wise of our Lord to use the example of sparrows! He could have used eagles. Or hawks, or falcons, or wide-winged storks. Yet out of the world's nine thousand bird species, the Lord chose one of the most insignificant, least noticed birds flying around. A scruffy little sparrow.

Jesus obviously wanted to make His point clear. Those who believe and follow Him mean more to the Father than anything else. If God takes note of each humble sparrow, where they are and what they're doing, you'd better believe He keeps tabs on you.

"Do not be afraid, little flock," Jesus tells us, "for your Father has been pleased to give you the kingdom" (Luke 12:32).

So are you anxious? Assaulted by fears, worry, and doubt? If the great God of Heaven concerns Himself with the little sparrow clinging to a twig outside your window, He cares about what concerns you.

Lord, I pour out my anxiety before you today.
You know of the concerns I have, and I know I
have nothing to lose but my fear by turning them
over to you. Thank you for meeting me right
where I am.

*H*ow great is the love the Father has lavished on
us, that we should be called children of God! And
that is what we are!

1 JOHN 3:1

*T*herefore, as God's chosen people, holy and dearly
loved, clothe yourselves with compassion, kindness,
humility, gentleness and patience.

COLOSSIANS 3:12

S *trengthen the feeble hands,*
       steady the knees that gave way;
say to those with fearful hearts,
       "Be strong, do not fear;
your God will come."

ISAIAH 35:3-4

Y *ou, O Lord, are a compassionate and gracious God.*

PSALM 86:15

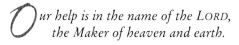

*O*ur help is in the name of the L*ORD*,
  the Maker of heaven and earth.

PSALM 124:8

*J*esus said, "I tell you the truth, if you have faith as
  small as a mustard seed, you can say to this mountain,
'Move from here to there' and it will move. Nothing will
be impossible for you."

MATTHEW 17:20

A LIST OF TEARS

*T*hink of all the tears you've cried. That time at recess when you weren't picked for dodgeball. The Saturday night of the prom when you sat home alone. The job interview that went sour. The time your neighbor told you to "quit talking about religion." The day your father died. The day your spouse left.

You may have thought no one noticed your red eyes. But God saw! What's more, he has every intention of rewarding your endurance through that pain. Why else would he meticulously chronicle every one of your tears (Psalm 56:8).

Every tear you've cried will be redeemed. God will give you indescribable glory for your grief, not with a general wave of the hand, but in a considered and specific way. Each tear has been listed; each will be recompensed.

I've cried a few times over not having use of my hands. I think it's ironic that on the day in heaven when I finally get back use of my hands so I can dry my own tears ... I won't have to: "He will wipe every tear from [our]eyes" (Revelation 21:4).

A CURE

There was a time during the early years of my paralysis when I could not even bring myself to talk about the depression that overwhelmed me. I did nothing. I said nothing. The look on my face was one of sullen, numb despair. I felt strangled by the cords of a living death, just as it says in Psalm 116:3. I didn't even care if there was a cure for my depression.

Thank God, there was a cure. Several friends met with my church youth leader every week to pray specifically for me, asking God to push back the darkness. Changes did not happen overnight, but slowly my countenance began to brighten. God was using prayers of my friends to sever the cords of deathly despair that entangled me. Praise God for friends who are willing to call on the name of the Lord on my behalf!

If you are feeling slump-shouldered today, call on the name of the Lord and ask him to save you. Remember, you may feel overcome by trouble and sorrow, but he who has overcome the world can deliver you.

The Spirit helps us in our weakness. We do not know what we ought to pray for, but the Spirit himself intercedes for us with groans that words cannot express.
ROMANS 8:26

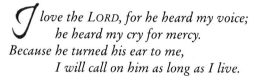

I love the LORD, for he heard my voice;
he heard my cry for mercy.
Because he turned his ear to me,
I will call on him as long as I live.

PSALM 116:1-2

I wait for you, O LORD;
you will answer, O Lord my God.

PSALM 38:15

*The eyes of the Lord are on the righteous
and his ears are attentive to their prayer.*

1 PETER 3:12

*Jesus said, "Surely I am with you always, to the very
end of the age."*

MATTHEW 28:20

RELY ON GOD

One summer, my family and I traveled to see a gigantic wonder called Carlsbad Caverns. I clasped my mother's hand as the tour guide led us down into the cavern. When we reached the bottom, our tour guide turned out the lamps so we could see, just for a moment, how thick the darkness really was.

I gasped as oppressive and utter blackness enveloped me. Panic seized me and I thrust my hand into the darkness to reach for my mother. In an instant her hand was around mine, washing away my fear and anxiety, "Joni," she said, "you're safe. I would never lose you."

You probably have days that seem like cavernous holes. You can't find your way and you search in vain for a single ray of light. Don't be alarmed! Remember that your walk is not by sight, but by faith. And God, according to Isaiah 50:10, agrees with you: There are times when it's hard to see even a single ray of brightness in your circumstances. But even in the blackness, God promises you will find him, close by. He says, "You're safe. I would never lose you!"

HEAL ME

$\mathcal{I}$n the early days of my injury my father would come to the hospital every day and whisper to me with wet eyes, "In every day and in every way, you're getting better and better and better." He'd say it every time he came.

But my body never did shake off the paralysis. The pragmatist would say, "See, your father's words were wishful thinking. You didn't get better, Joni; instead, you got stuck with a wheelchair."

That's not the way I choose to look at it. Daddy was right. Every day I did get better. Maybe not on the outside, but on the inside. My soul became settled. My hope became clear. This is the sort of healing described in Jeremiah 17:14—"Heal me, O LORD, and I will be healed; save me and I will be saved, for you are the one I praise." God is interested in healing the inside of a person. For me, a healed and happy heart is the best "better"—by a long shot.

"*I know the plans I have for you,*" *declares the* LORD, "*plans to prosper you and not to harm you, plans to give you hope and a future. You will call on me and come and pray to me, and I will listen to you. You will seek me and find me when you seek me with all your heart.*"

JEREMIAH 29:11-13

I call to God,
　　and the LORD *saves me.*
Evening, morning and noon
　　I cry out in distress,
　　and he hears my voice.

PSALM 55:16-17

SOURCES

All excerpts were taken from the following books by Joni Eareckson Tada

Diamonds in the Dust. Grand Rapids, MI: Zondervan, 1993.

Heaven. Grand Rapids, MI: Zondervan, 1995.

More Precious Than Silver. Grand Rapids, MI: Zondervan, 1998.

NIV Encouragement Bible, New International Bible. General Editors: Tada, Joni Eareckson and Dravecky, Dave and Jan. Zondervan: Grand Rapids, MI., 2001.

Secret Strength. Sisters, OR: Multnomah Books, 1994.